by Terry Collins

illustrated by Kelly Brown

CONSULTANT:

Kenneth E. deGraffenreid
Professor of Intelligence Studies
Institute of World Politics
Washington, D.C.

Mankato, Minnesota

Graphic Library is published by Capstone Press,
151 Good Counsel Drive, P.O. Box 669, Mankato, Minnesota 56002.
www.capstonepress.com

1 2 3 4 5 6 13 12 11 10 09 08

Library of Congress Cataloging-in-Publication Data
Collins, Terry.
    The FBI / by Terry Collins; illustrated by Kelly Brown.
    p. cm. — (Graphic library. Cartoon nation)
    Summary: "In cartoon format, explains the history of the FBI and describes the duties
and responsibilities of FBI special agents" — Provided by publisher.
    Includes bibliographical references and index.
    ISBN-13: 978-1-4296-1982-0 (hardcover)
    ISBN-10: 1-4296-1982-1 (hardcover)
    ISBN-13: 978-1-4296-2854-9 (softcover pbk.)
    ISBN-10: 1-4296-2854-5 (softcover pbk.)
    1. United States. Federal Bureau of Investigation — Juvenile literature. 2. Criminal
investigation — United States — Juvenile literature. I. Brown, Kelly, ill. II. Title. III. Title:
Federal Bureau of Investigation. IV. Series.
HV8144.F43C65 2009
363.250973 — dc22   2008000506

Art Director and Designer
Bob Lentz

Production Designer
Kim Brown

Editor
Christopher L. Harbo

Photo illustration credits: Wikimedia Commons, 17

TABLE OF CONTENTS

★ Very Special Agents.................... **4**

★ Secret Origins........................ **6**

★ Gangsters and G-Men.................. **8**

★ The Hoover Years..................... **10**

★ A World at War **12**

★ Atomic Spies **14**

★ The FBI After 9/11 .... **16**

★ Today's FBI **18**

★ The Right Stuff...................... **20**

★ Tools of the Trade................... **22**

★ Canine Crime Busters................. **24**

★ A Day On the Job.................... **26**

Time Line   28
Glossary.   30
Read More   31
Internet Sites   31
Index   32

The Federal Bureau of Investigation (FBI) is one of the most famous law enforcement agencies in the world. It defends the United States against violence, crime, fraud, **espionage**, and other national threats.

espionage — the actions of a spy to gain sensitive national, political, or economic information

Many people think of FBI special agents as spies, but they're not. The FBI keeps people safe in the United States and catches foreign spies. The Central Intelligence Agency (CIA) handles spying and other tasks outside of the United States.

The world of the FBI isn't as exciting as you see on TV. Special agents rarely draw their weapons or get into car chases. Agents spend much of their time investigating crimes, collecting evidence, and writing reports.

People work in many kinds of jobs with the FBI. Some people work with computers, while others translate languages. Mechanics, nurses, teachers, and dozens of other workers are also a part of the bureau.

However, the special agent is the best-known job in the FBI. These men and women investigate crimes where they take place. Let's see how these special agents and the FBI got their start.

CLOSE TO HOME

FBI Headquarters are located in Washington, D.C. There are 56 field offices located in major cities, such as New York, Los Angeles, and Atlanta. Smaller towns across the country host more than 400 local FBI agencies.

In 1908, President Theodore Roosevelt was worried about the increase of crime across the United States. Attorney General Charles Bonaparte had the answer. Bonaparte created a group of 10 agents who worked only for the Department of Justice.

These 10 men went after criminals who crossed state lines. Before this time, local police had to stop the chase if a suspect left their state. The new government agents could go anywhere in the country.

On July 26, 1908, these "special agents" were assigned to Chief Examiner Stanley W. Fitch. This day was the beginning of the FBI.

The newly named Bureau of Investigation (BOI) looked into crimes involving banking and land fraud. As the responsibilities of the BOI grew, so did its numbers. By 1920, more than 300 special agents worked with the bureau.

We gotta find a bigger office!

When the United States entered World War I in 1917, the bureau's duties grew even more. President Woodrow Wilson ordered the BOI to arrest illegal immigrants to stop enemy spies on American shores.

Me? A spy? What gave me away?

ON-THE-JOB TRAINING

In the early days, the BOI provided no training to agents. Previous police experience was preferred, but many agents had backgrounds as lawyers or accountants instead.

After World War I ended in 1918, crime in the United States rose sharply. When the legal sale of liquor was banned, criminals stepped in to supply alcohol. By 1930, bank robbers and **bootleggers** pushed local police forces to the limit. Soon, gangsters began working on a national level. The Bureau of Investigation became involved in a war on crime.

You're not so tough — OW!

It's all in the badge.

You? Good looking? Please! I'm the "Pretty Boy," remember?

A "Baby Face" beats a mug like yours any day of the week!

The battle was on. Gangster John Dillinger earned the rank of "public enemy #1" for his crimes. Crooks with colorful names like "Pretty Boy" Floyd and "Baby Face" Nelson appeared in newspapers. The kidnapping of the son of famed airplane pilot Charles Lindbergh caused Congress to increase the power of the bureau.

bootlegger — a person who sells illegally made alcohol or liquor

The need for a national crime-fighting unit became serious after the Kansas City Massacre. On June 17, 1933, four law enforcement members were killed, including BOI agent Raymond Caffery. The American people were ready for the government to take action against crime.

On September 26, 1933, the BOI cornered kidnapper and bank robber George "Machine Gun" Kelly in Memphis, Tennessee. Kelly gave up without firing a single shot. Instead, he gave the agents the nickname of "G-Men" (short for "Government Men").

Don't shoot, G-Men, don't shoot!

Hey, that's a catchy name!

I like it!

AL CAPONE

ALWAYS PAY YOUR TAXES

Al "Scarface" Capone was an infamous gangster of the 1920s. Despite efforts by the BOI and local law enforcement to arrest him, Capone remained free. Finally in 1931, he was arrested and sent to prison for not paying his income taxes.

Legendary crime-buster J. Edgar Hoover was born in Washington, D.C., in 1895. Joining the BOI in 1917, Hoover quickly worked his way up the ranks. He became director in 1924 at the age of 29. He remained in the job until his death on May 2, 1972.

Immediately, tough-minded Hoover shaped the bureau into his vision for the agency. Hoover was so tough on crime, many joked that his first initial "J" stood for "Justice."

His first name was actually John.

Hoover wanted only the best special agents on his team. He set up interviews, background checks, and physical fitness tests for all applicants. He also believed in the power of science. He helped create a special bureau laboratory division to look at criminal evidence.

One, two, three . . . do those jumping jacks faster!

But Mr. Hoover, I'm a scientist, not a field agent.

FIT TO PRINT

Hoover established a national registry of fingerprints to share with other law enforcement agencies. This FBI database is now the largest collection of fingerprints in the world.

In 1935, Hoover wanted to change the name of the agency to match the growing powers of his agents. A suggestion to add the word "Federal" to "Bureau of Investigation" stuck.

The FBI. A new name for a new organization!

The United States entered World War II in 1941. The FBI's task was to keep the nation's borders and shores safe from invasion.

All clear here. And the water feels fine!

Meanwhile, a German terrorist plot was brewing. Eight Germans planned to destroy water supplies and use bombs in public places. The first four **terrorists** arrived in Long Island, New York, on June 13, 1942. Learning of the plot, the FBI launched a secret manhunt to find the spies.

terrorist — someone who uses violence and threats to frighten people into obeying

Fearing discovery, one of the four Germans surrendered at the FBI Headquarters in Washington, D.C. When questioned, he said that four more spies were in Florida.

Within days, the FBI had the Long Island spies in custody. By June 27, 1942, all four members of the Florida group were behind bars too. The arrests had been so quick that none of the eight men had time to commit a single crime.

GOING SOUTH

In 1940, the FBI created a Special Intelligence Service (SIS) to allow agents to work outside of the United States. From Mexico City to Brazil, the SIS worked with local governments to keep German agents and smugglers out of North and South America.

On August 29, 1949, the skies over a weapons test site in Kazakhstan went white. The Soviet Union had tested its first atomic bomb. In the United States, scientists were puzzled. Until then, only America had nuclear weapons.

There was only one answer: a traitor gave **classified secrets** to the Soviets. The FBI went on alert. This case was a matter of national security. Director Hoover was determined not to fail.

classified secret — sensitive information that will cause damage to national security if released

May I help you?

What do you know about stolen nuclear secrets?

Bureau agents traveled to Los Alamos, New Mexico. They checked employee backgrounds at the nuclear weapons testing site. They also asked questions about suspicious behavior. The investigation took several months. Finally, in June 1950, agents had a suspect — David Greenglass.

Greenglass was arrested as a spy with ties to Los Alamos. Along with Greenglass, the FBI locked up his wife, Ruth. To save himself, Greenglass gave the names of his sister and brother-in-law, Ethel and Julius Rosenberg.

ETHEL AND JULIUS ROSENBERG

The investigation uncovered the spy ring's methods. Seeking more traitors, the Justice Department asked for the death penalty for the Rosenbergs. FBI Director Hoover hoped they would name others involved to avoid the death penalty.

But the Rosenbergs stayed silent. On June 19, 1953, the married spies were executed. In a rare setback for the FBI, neither of the Rosenbergs ever gave the names of their Soviet contacts.

CRACKING THE CODE

FBI special agent Robert Lamphere assisted in cracking the codes for several secret Soviet messages. One of these codes revealed that Klaus Fuchs, a British scientist, was a spy. Fuchs' capture and confession gave the name of David Greenglass and led to the end of the Rosenberg spy ring.

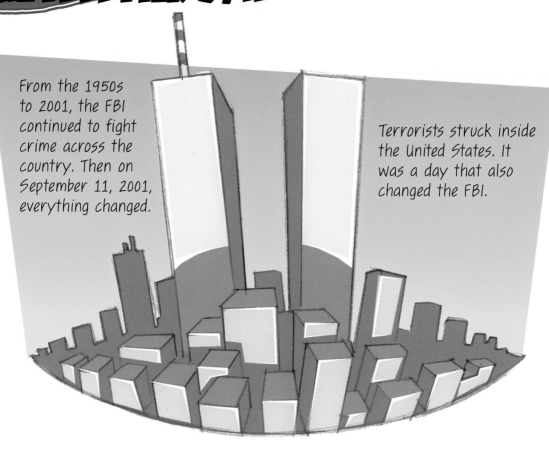

From the 1950s to 2001, the FBI continued to fight crime across the country. Then on September 11, 2001, everything changed.

Terrorists struck inside the United States. It was a day that also changed the FBI.

The terrorist attacks took the lives of more than 3,000 people. The attack and crash sites were the largest crime scenes in FBI history.

At the peak of the 9/11 investigation, more than half of all FBI agents were working on this case. These agents followed more than half a million leads.

After 9/11, the FBI's top priority shifted from organized and public crime. Now it focuses on protecting America from terrorist attacks. The FBI's mission is simple:

Never again to allow an act of terror to happen on American soil.

WHAT DOES IT ALL MEAN?

Adopted in 1940, all of the colors in the FBI Seal carry special meaning.

Blue represents justice.

Red stands for courage, bravery, and strength.

White means cleanliness, light, truth, and peace.

Gold stands for the highest values of the agency.

The FBI has changed a lot since it was founded in 1908. Today's FBI is made up of an investigations force that oversees more than 200 types of federal law. The major types are grouped into eight units. Three units involve national security and five focus on criminal activity.

NATIONAL SECURITY PRIORITIES

1. COUNTERTERRORISM: STOPPING TERRORISM BEFORE IT STARTS

This unit keeps a close watch on worldwide and American-based terrorist groups. The counterterrorism section also tracks the movement of weapons.

2. COUNTERINTELLIGENCE: KEEPING OUR SECRETS SECURE

Counterintelligence protects top-secret information. Agents figure out what enemies want to steal and how they would do it. Their goal is to stop the crime before it happens.

3. CYBER CRIME: CYBERSPACE SHOULD BE CYBER-SAFE

The cyber unit prevents computer viruses, identifies online predators, and stops copyright theft. It also keeps organized crime from committing Internet fraud.

CRIMINAL PRIORITIES

4. PUBLIC CORRUPTION: ABUSE OF TRUST

Crooked politicians are bad news. They take bribes, steal money, and lie to voters. Our government is kept honest by the public corruption unit.

5. CIVIL RIGHTS: EVERYONE IS EQUAL

The FBI works side-by-side with local law enforcement to stop all forms of hate crimes.

6. WHITE-COLLAR CRIME: FRAUD

This unit investigates insurance fraud, identity theft, and credit card scams. These crimes are known as "white-collar" crimes because no weapons are used.

7. ORGANIZED CRIME: MORE THAN THE MAFIA

Besides the Italian Mafia, the FBI monitors Russian mobsters, Chinese tongs, and other crime rings in the United States.

8. MAJOR THEFT / VIOLENT CRIME: ON THE STREETS

Special agents work closely with state and local partners to solve bank robberies, thefts, and murders.

To fight terrorism and crime, the FBI looks for talented citizens between the ages of 23 and 36. These men and women must be college graduates with at least three years of professional work experience in any field. They must also pass a physical fitness test.

You call that a push-up?

Other than aspirin, you're drug free.

All FBI jobs require a top secret security clearance. This clearance is given only after a series of lengthy background checks, including drug use and previous arrests.

Candidates must pass a lie detector test. In the FBI, honesty is always the best policy.

What do you mean you forgot your name?

I'm sorry. I'm nervous, okay?

Finally, detailed interviews are held with former employers, friends, neighbors, teachers, and relatives to check the candidate's background.

Once all the checks are done, a special agent candidate must qualify for one of five entry programs:

- Accounting
- Computer Science/Information Technology
- Language
- Law
- Diversified (All other jobs)

TRAINING DAYS

New special agents go to the FBI Academy in Quantico, Virginia, for 17 weeks of training. During this time, they live on-campus. The FBI Academy course of study includes:

Federal Law	Scientific Criminal
Interviewing Techniques	Investigation
Crime Scene Analysis	Surveillance
Computer Skills	Defensive Tactics
Counterintelligence	Firearm Use

FBI agents use the best in modern **technology** to help with their jobs. From hidden cameras to fingerprint scanners, special agents use many gadgets to make life easier and safer.

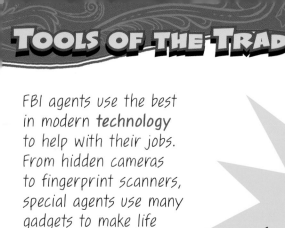

> I'm fully equipped, but I can't move!

Many of these gadgets use radio signals to help with eavesdropping. These tiny listening devices are better known as "bugs." They can be easily hidden and are very useful in gathering evidence for a case.

> I think this bug is broken, sir.

> Rookies!

technology — the use of science to do practical things, such as designing complex machines

Hidden cameras are another FBI tool. Some of these cameras can recognize faces. These cameras use information such as nose width and cheekbone shape to create a "faceprint." The gathered information can be compared to other photos on a computer.

Even fingerprinting has gone high-tech. Special scanners can compare a single fingerprint to millions on file in the FBI's Integrated Automated Fingerprint Identification System (IAFIS). Agents use these hand-held scanners in the field.

WORD-PLAY

Many FBI agents use slang terms when talking among themselves:

Beach Time: an agent who is suspended

Rent-A-Goons: agents loaned out to assist in another FBI field office

Creds: FBI badge and identification

Brick Agent: an FBI field agent

Dry Cleaning: attempt to detect being followed or watched

Tailed: being followed

Some of the most valued FBI members are the trained dogs who help fight crime. These four-legged officers have an amazing sense of smell. In fact, this powerful sense of smell takes up nearly one-eighth of a dog's brain!

N-n-nice doggie!

Now that's what I call playing fetch!

WOOF!

Teamed up with a human handler, FBI dogs sniff out bombs, guns, money, drugs, and even criminal suspects. Handlers teach their canine partners how to find items even under tough weather conditions.

Dogs have 44 times the smelling power of humans. They can pick up a scent from more than half a mile away under good weather conditions.

Okay, I promise. No more liver and onion sandwiches on duty.

THE DOG POUND

A variety of dogs with different abilities serve the FBI. Here are some real life examples of heroic dogs that help make our country safe every day.

Axel

German Shepherd/ Rottweiler Mix

In 1997, Axel found a total of $25 million worth of illegal drugs.

Drago

Dutch Shepherd

When Drago finds a lost person, he lies down and barks.

Power

Labrador Retriever

Power is able to sniff out 19,000 different explosive components.

The life of an FBI special agent is different every day. One shift might find an agent busy searching for evidence. The next day could be spent in the office writing reports.

Yeah, I'm staking out the ski slopes in Colorado for the rest of the week.

Nice!

FBI special agents make sure their investigations are accurate before making an arrest. Capturing a suspect is often easy and goes without problems. But making a case that will hold up in court is the hard part of the job.

Nice work. I don't even know why I came along.

Because we're using your car.

Listening to recorded conversations takes many hours. These talks are recorded with hidden bugs. Special agents must write down everything that is said for use as evidence in a trial.

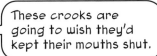

These crooks are going to wish they'd kept their mouths shut.

An agent never stays still long enough to get comfortable. A large part of the job is street work. Special agents go to crime scenes and interview witnesses.

I told you I don't need any magazines!

I'm not selling anything, sir. I'm an FBI special agent.

Life in the FBI is challenging, but never boring. And best of all, the men and women who carry FBI badges go home each night knowing they are serving their country.

Wait, I want to learn more!

Then go to our Web site. See you tomorrow at the FBI Academy.

TIME LINE

1908 — President Theodore Roosevelt requests a team of agents to work for the Department of Justice. This is the beginning of the FBI.

1908

1924 — J. Edgar Hoover is named Director of the Bureau of Investigation (BOI). He serves in this post until his death in 1972.

1924

1950 — The FBI's Ten Most Wanted Fugitives program begins.

1950

1972 — The new FBI Academy is opened on the U.S. Marine Corps base in Quantico, Virginia.

1972

1978 — The use of lasers to detect fingerprints begins.

1978

1932 — The crime-solving
FBI laboratory is created.

1934 — Legendary
gangster John Dillinger,
known as "public enemy
#1," is killed by FBI
agents in Chicago.

1932

1940 — The FBI Disaster
Squad is created to identify
bodies after airline disasters.

1934

1940

Disaster Strikes

2001 — After the World
Trade Center and Pentagon
attacks, the FBI makes fighting
terrorism its top priority.

1983 — The FBI Hostage
Rescue Team is established,
acting to save lives in crisis
across the United States.

1983

2001

GLOSSARY

bootlegger (BOOT-leger) — a person who sells illegally made alcohol or liquor

classified secret (KLAH-suh-fide SEE-krit) — sensitive information that will cause damage to national security if released

corruption (kuh-RUP-shuhn) — dishonest behavior

custody (KUHS-tuh-dee) — arrested by the police

database (DAY-tuh-bays) — a collection of organized information on a computer

espionage (ESS-pee-uh-nahzh) — the actions of a spy to gain sensitive national, political, or economic information

fraud (FRAWD) — the practice of cheating or tricking people

gangster (GANG-stur) — a member of a criminal gang

illegal immigrant (i-LEE-guhl IM-uh-gruhnt) — a foreign-born person living in a country without legal permission

investigation (in-vess-tuh-GAY-shuhn) — the act of searching for facts to solve a crime

surrender (suh-REN-dur) — to give up or admit defeat

technology (tek-NOL-uh-jee) — the use of science to do practical things, such as designing complex machines

terrorist (TER-uhr-ist) — someone who uses violence and threats to frighten people into obeying

traitor (TRAY-tuhr) — someone who turns against his or her country

READ MORE

Baker, David. *CIA & FBI.* Fighting Terrorism. Vero Beach, Fla.: Rourke, 2006.

Hamilton, John. *The FBI.* Defending the Nation. Edina, Minn.: ABDO, 2007.

Karlitz, Gail. *Virtual Apprentice: FBI Agent.* New York: Ferguson, 2007.

Miller, Connie Colwell. *The Federal Bureau of Investigation: Hunting Criminals.* Line of Duty. Mankato, Minn.: Capstone Press, 2008.

Wagner, Heather Lehr. *The Federal Bureau of Investigation.* The U.S. Government. New York: Chelsea House, 2007.

INTERNET SITES

FactHound offers a safe, fun way to find Internet sites related to this book. All of the sites on FactHound have been researched by our staff.

Here's how:
1. Visit *www.facthound.com*
2. Choose your grade level.
3. Type in this book ID 1429619821 for age-appropriate sites. You may also browse subjects by clicking on letters, or by clicking on pictures and words.
4. Click on the Fetch It button.

FactHound will fetch the best sites for you!

INDEX

Bonaparte, Charles, 6

Caffery, Raymond, 9
Central Intelligence Agency
    (CIA), 4

Department of Justice, 6, 15, 28
dogs, 24–25

Federal Bureau of Investigation
    (FBI)
    FBI Academy, 21, 27, 28
    FBI Disaster Squad, 29
    FBI Hostage Rescue
        Team, 29
    FBI Laboratory, 11, 29
    field offices, 5, 23
    Headquarters, 5, 13
    investigation priorities,
        18–19
    names, 7, 11
    origins, 6–7, 28
    seal, 17
fingerprints, 11, 22, 23, 28
Fitch, Stanley W., 6

gangsters, 8–9
    Capone, Al "Scarface," 9
    Dillinger, John, 8, 29
    Floyd, "Pretty Boy," 8
    Kelly, George "Machine
        Gun," 9
    Nelson, "Baby Face," 8

Hoover, J. Edgar, 10–11, 14,
    15, 28

Kansas City Massacre, 9

Lamphere, Robert, 15
Lindbergh, Charles, 8

Quantico, Virginia, 21, 28

Roosevelt, Theodore, 6, 28

September 11 attacks, 16–17, 29
slang, 23
special agents
    daily life, 5, 26–27
    nicknames, 9
    qualifications, 20
    testing, 11, 20–21
    tools, 22–23
    training, 7, 21
Special Intelligence Service
    (SIS), 13
spies, 4, 7, 12–13, 14–15
    Fuchs, Klaus, 15
    Greenglass, David, 14–15
    Rosenberg, Ethel, 15
    Rosenberg, Julius, 15

Ten Most Wanted List, 28
terrorists, 12–13, 16–17, 18, 29

Wilson, Woodrow, 7